W9-CGR-664

Fact Finders™

Questions and Answers: Countries

Spain

A Question and Answer Book

by Kremena Spengler

Consultant:
James D. Fernández
Chair, Department of Spanish and Portuguese
Director, King Juan Carlos I of Spain Center
New York University, New York

Capstone
press

Mankato, Minnesota

Fact Finders is published by Capstone Press,
151 Good Counsel Drive, P.O. Box 669, Mankato, Minnesota 56002.
www.capstonepress.com

Library of Congress Cataloging-in-Publication Data
Spengler, Kremena.
     Spain : a question and answer book / by Kremena Spengler.
     p. cm.—(Fact finders. Questions and answers. Countries)
     Summary: "Describes the geography, history, economy, and culture of Spain in a
     question-and-answer format"–Provided by publisher.
     Includes bibliographical references and index.
     ISBN 0–7368–4357–4 (hardcover)
     1. Spain—Miscellanea—Juvenile literature. I. Title. II. Series.
DP17.S684 2006
946—dc22   2005001235

Editorial Credits
Silver Editions, editorial, design, and production; Kia Adams, set designer; Ortelius Design,
Inc., cartographer; Wanda Winch, photo researcher; Scott Thoms, photo editor

Photo Credits
Art Directors/George Taylor, 18–19, 23; Robert Belbin, 11
Capstone Press Archives, 29 (bill, coin)
Corbis/Francesco Muntada, 4; Nik Wheeler, 13; Reuters, 8
Getty Images Inc./AFP/Pierre Philippe Marcou, 8–9; Newsmakers/Carlos Alvarez, 7
Index Stock Imagery/HIRB, 17
One Mile Up, Inc., 29 (flag)
Richard T. Nowitz, 21
Woodfin Camp & Associates, Inc./Kim Newton, 25; Robert Frerck, cover (background,
foreground), 1, 15, 27

Artistic Effects:
Corel, 12
Ingram Publishing, 16
Photodisc/C Squared Studios, 20; PhotoLink, 24

1 2 3 4 5 6 10 09 08 07 06 05

Table of Contents

Where is Spain?. 4

When did Spain become a country? 6

What type of government does Spain have? 8

What kind of housing does Spain have? 10

What are Spain's forms of transportation? 12

What are Spain's major industries?. 14

What is school like in Spain?. 16

What are Spain's favorite sports and games? 18

What are the traditional art forms in Spain? 20

What major holidays do people in Spain celebrate? 22

What are the traditional foods of Spain? 24

What is family life like in Spain? 26

Features

Spain Fast Facts. 28

Money and Flag. 29

Learn to Speak Spanish 30

Glossary 30

Internet Sites. 31

Read More 31

Index 32

Where is Spain?

Spain covers most of the Iberian **Peninsula** in southwestern Europe. Spain is about twice the size of Oregon.

The Balearic Islands in the Mediterranean Sea are part of Spain. So are the Canary Islands off the coast of Africa in the Atlantic Ocean.

Small villages can be found throughout the Pyrenees Mountains.

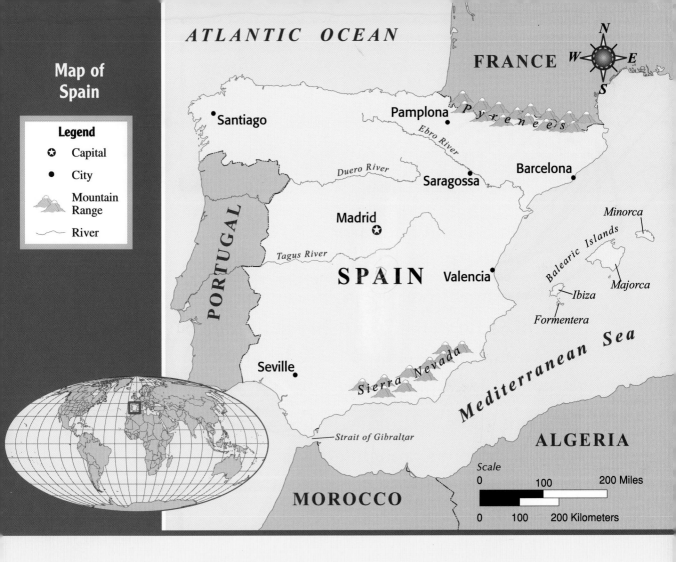

Map of Spain

Legend
- ✪ Capital
- • City
- ⛰ Mountain Range
- ∼ River

ATLANTIC OCEAN

FRANCE

• Santiago

Pamplona •

Pyrenees

Ebro River

Duero River

Saragossa •

Barcelona •

Madrid ✪

Tagus River

SPAIN

Valencia •

Minorca

Balearic Islands

Majorca

Ibiza

Formentera

PORTUGAL

Seville •

Sierra Nevada

Mediterranean Sea

ALGERIA

Strait of Gibraltar

Scale

0   100   200 Miles

0   100   200 Kilometers

MOROCCO

The Pyrenees Mountains in the north form the border with France. Coastal plains run along the Atlantic Ocean and the Mediterranean Sea.

Most of Spain has hot, dry summers and cold winters. Coastal areas are milder.

When did Spain become a country?

Spain became a country in 1492. Until then, Greeks, Romans, and others ruled the area. Muslims from North Africa took over most of Spain in the 700s. Christians fought against the Muslims for 700 years. They ended Muslim rule in 1492.

In the 1500s, Spain ruled Mexico and Peru. Spanish explorers brought gold to Spain. As these riches ran out, Spain lost its power.

Fact!

Before he died, General Francisco Franco named Spain's next leader, King Juan Carlos I. Most Spanish people highly respect King Juan Carlos I. He helped keep Spain peaceful after Franco's death.

King Juan Carlos I (center) and members of the royal family attend a ceremony to celebrate Spanish literature.

In 1936, Spain's military rose up against the government. This started the Spanish civil war. It lasted from 1936 to 1939. Military forces led by General Francisco Franco won the war. Franco ruled Spain until his death in 1975. King Juan Carlos I became the next leader of Spain.

What type of government does Spain have?

Spain's government is a **constitutional monarchy**. The chief of state is the king. He represents the country at events. The king's powers are limited.

A **prime minister** leads the government. The prime minister chooses other ministers who run parts of the government.

King Juan Carlos I waves to a crowd during a visit to the United States.

Spain's parliament, the Cortes, listened to King Juan Carlos I (standing by flag) in 2003.

Spain's **parliament**, the Cortes, makes the country's laws. It also chooses the prime minister. The parliament includes the Congress of Deputies and the Senate. It meets in Spain's capital, Madrid.

What kind of housing does Spain have?

People who live in large Spanish cities prefer apartments to houses. Some own very large apartments. Others own smaller apartments in high-rise buildings. Many city people also have weekend houses in rural areas or near the sea.

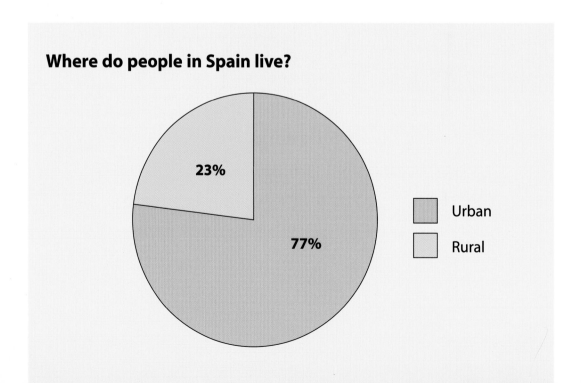

Where do people in Spain live?

23%

77%

Urban

Rural

White farmhouses are common in southern Spain.

People in small towns often live in town houses. Many of these houses have three floors. The living area is on the upper two floors. A garage is on the ground floor.

Houses in the south are built of clay. Small windows keep the inside cool.

What are Spain's forms of transportation?

Spain has road, rail, air, and water transportation. Most families have a car. In Madrid and other cities, people also take buses and the subway. Most goods are shipped on trucks and trains. Spanish airlines have many flights to other Spanish-speaking countries in Latin America.

Fact!

In the past, Spain's many mountains made it difficult to build roads. People used horses and other animals to carry goods.

Long lines of cars often cause heavy traffic in cities such as Barcelona.

Water transportation has developed along Spain's long coastline. About 200 ports are located along the Atlantic Ocean and the Mediterranean Sea.

What are Spain's major industries?

Most Spaniards have jobs in **service industries**. They work in hotels, banks, shops, and other businesses.

Tourism is a large service industry in Spain. More than 50 million tourists visit the country each year. Visitors stay at hotels on the southern coast or the Spanish islands. They also explore the country's old towns, castles, and museums.

What does Spain import and export?

Imports	Exports
aircraft	automobiles
chemicals	clothing
consumer goods	footwear
fish	fruits

At a factory in Barcelona, many machines are needed to put the body of a car together.

Spanish factories make many goods. Some make clothes, shoes, and food. Others make ships or cars.

Farming in Spain is smaller than other industries. Farmers grow vegetables, olives, grapes, and citrus fruits. Others raise animals.

What is school like in Spain?

Students in Spain must attend grade school from age 6 to 13. Then they attend high school from age 14 to 16. After age 16, some students take courses to get ready for college. Others learn job skills.

Fact!

Spain has a long school day. Grade school students go to school from 9:00 in the morning to 1:00 in the afternoon. Then they take a long break for lunch. During this time, all schools are closed. Schools re-open at 3:00 until 5:00 in the afternoon.

A group of middle school students read and discuss a bulletin board.

Most children attend free public schools. Some students attend private schools. Most private schools in Spain are Catholic.

After high school, students can take a test to attend a college. Colleges offer classes in art, science, law, and many other fields.

What are Spain's favorite sports and games?

Many Spaniards like soccer. Soccer is called *fútbol* in Spain. Almost every town has a soccer field and a team. Townspeople cheer for their local teams. They also cheer for one of two main professional teams, Real Madrid or FC Barcelona. These clubs are among the best in Europe.

Fact!

Spain's Basque people play a game called pelota. Players use a special glove to hit a rubber ball off a wall. Some people say it is the fastest game in the world.

A matador steps aside as a bull charges during a bullfight.

Bullfighting is a well-known Spanish sport. Fighters called picadors first weaken the bull. Then the main bullfighter, the matador, uses his cape to draw the bull as close to him as possible. He must be careful not to get hurt or killed by the bull. In the end, the matador kills the bull.

What are the traditional art forms in Spain?

Many major works of art were created in the 1600s. This time is known as the Golden Age. In the 1600s, El Greco and Diego Velázquez created famous paintings. Miguel de Cervantes wrote *Don Quixote.*

In the 1900s, Spanish painters included Pablo Picasso and Salvador Dalí. They became famous for their modern art.

Fact!

The guitar was invented in Spain in the 1500s. It is related to the lute (right), an instrument that was brought to Spain by the Moors.

Flamenco dancers perform at a night club in Seville.

Flamenco is a traditional type of music in Spain. The three parts of flamenco are song, dance, and guitar. Flamenco singers tell deep feelings with their singing. People in the audience may clap their hands, snap their fingers, or stomp their feet.

What major holidays do people in Spain celebrate?

Spain celebrates National Day on October 12. On that date in 1492, Christopher Columbus first reached America. On National Day, businesses and schools are closed. The military holds parades.

Each town in Spain has a celebration called a **fiesta**. Fiestas honor saints or the changing seasons. They may last a week.

What other holidays do people in Spain celebrate?

Christmas Day
Day of the Constitution
Epiphany
Feast of the Assumption
May Day/Labor Day
New Year's Day

Bulls charge toward the bullring during the bull running in Falces.

A famous fiesta in Pamplona in July honors Saint Fermín. Local people release bulls from pens outside town. The bulls run through the streets to the bullring.

What are the traditional foods of Spain?

Spanish meals usually include meat or seafood with vegetables and fruit. Beans, lentils, chickpeas, and rice are also common. Spanish food is often cooked with olive oil and garlic.

Fact!

The people of Spain eat more fresh fish than any other country except for Japan.

A woman prepares to serve paella, one of Spain's most popular dishes.

Paella is a famous Spanish dish. Paella is made of rice, meat, seafood, and vegetables.

Lunch is the main meal in Spain. Most Spaniards take a long lunch, from about 2:00 to 5:00 in the afternoon. Some take a siesta, or nap, after lunch.

What is family life like in Spain?

Spanish families are close. Relatives usually live in the same town and gather for meals on weekends. Grandparents help care for children. People often live with their parents until they get married.

What are Spain's ethnic groups by language?
(All people in Spain speak Castilian Spanish. Some people also speak regional languages.)

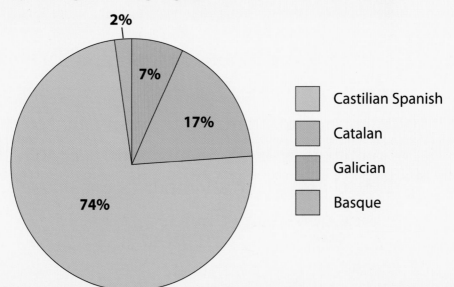

2%

7%

17%

74%

- Castilian Spanish
- Catalan
- Galician
- Basque

Spanish family members often gather to share a meal.

In many Spanish families, both parents work. In traditional families, the mother takes care of the home and children.

Spaniards keep their homes private. Friends meet at restaurants or cafés. People also take evening walks together.

Spain Fast Facts

Official name:

Kingdom of Spain

Land area:

*192,873 square miles
(499,542 square kilometers)*

**Average annual
precipitation:**

26 inches (66 centimeters)

**Average January
temperature (Madrid):**

*42 degrees Fahrenheit
(6 degrees Celsius)*

**Average July
temperature (Madrid):**

*76 degrees Fahrenheit
(24 degrees Celsius)*

Population:

40,280,780 people

Capital city:

Madrid

Languages:

*Castilian Spanish, Catalan,
Galician, Basque*

Natural resources:

*coal, copper, iron ore, lead,
mercury, uranium, zinc*

Religions:

Roman Catholic	*94%*
Other	*6%*

Money and Flag

Money:

Spain's money is the euro. In 2005, 1 U.S. dollar equaled 0.76 euro. One Canadian dollar equaled 0.61 euro.

Flag:

The red and yellow stripes on Spain's flag represent old Spanish kingdoms. The yellow stripe in the middle contains the national coat of arms. The coat of arms includes the royal seal. The seal is framed by the Pillars of Hercules.

Learn to Speak Spanish

Most people in Spain speak Castilian Spanish. It is Spain's official language. Learn to speak some Spanish words using the chart below.

English	Spanish	Pronunciation
yes	sí	(SEE)
no	no	(NOH)
hello	hola	(OH-lah)
good-bye	adiós	(ah-dee-OHS)
please	por favor	(POR-fa-VOR)
thank you	gracias	(GRAH-thee-ahs)
good morning	buenos días	(BWAY-nahs DEE-ahs)
good evening	buenas noches	(BWAY-nahs NO-chays)
How are you?	¿Cómo estás?	(KOH-moh ay-STAHS)

Glossary

constitutional monarchy (kon-sti-TOO-shun-uhl MON-ar-kee)—a system of government in which the monarch's powers are limited and there is a written system of laws

fiesta (fee-ES-tuh)—holiday or religious festival

flamenco (fluh-MEN-ko)—an art form in Spain that includes song, dance, and guitar

parliament (PAR-luh-muhnt)—the group of people who have been elected to make laws in some countries

peninsula (puh-NIN-suh-luh)—a piece of land that is surrounded by water on three sides

prime minister (PRIME MIN-uh-stur)—the person in charge of a government in some countries

service industries (SUR-viss IN-duh-streez)—businesses that help and take care of customers

Internet Sites

FactHound offers a safe, fun way to find Internet sites related to this book. All of the sites on FactHound have been researched by our staff.

Here's how:
1. Visit *www.facthound.com*
2. Type in this special code **0736843574** for age-appropriate sites. Or enter a search word related to this book for a more general search.
3. Click on the **Fetch It** button.

FactHound will fetch the best sites for you!

Read More

Bader, Philip. *Spain.* Dropping in on. Vero Beach, Fla.: Rourke Publishing, 2001.

Davis, Kevin. *Look What Came From Spain.* New York: Franklin Watts, 2002.

Deady, Kathleen W. *Spain.* Countries of the World. Mankato, Minn.: Bridgestone Books, 2001.

Yanuck, Debbie L. *Spain.* Many Cultures, One World. Mankato, Minn.: Blue Earth Books, 2004.

Index

agriculture, 15
art forms, 20–21

bullfighting, 19

capital. See Madrid
Cervantes, Miguel de, 20
climate, 5, 28
Columbus, Christopher, 22

Dalí, Salvador, 20

ethnic groups, 26
exports, 14

families, 12, 26–27
farming. See agriculture
flag, 29
flamenco, 21
food, 15, 24–25
Franco, Francisco, 6, 7

games, 18
government, 8–9
guitar, 20

history, 6–7
holidays, 22–23
housing, 10–11

imports, 14
industries, 14–15

Juan Carlos I, King, 6, 7, 8, 9

landforms, 4–5
language, 26, 28, 30

Madrid, 9, 12, 28
money, 29
music, 20–21

natural resources, 28

parliament, 9
pelota, 18
Picasso, Pablo, 20
population, 10, 28
prime minister, 8

religion, 17, 28

school, 16–17
sports, 18–19

transportation, 12–13

Velázquez, Diego, 20

weather. See climate